Fabulous Cakes and Desserts

by Norma Olizon-Chikiamco

Try a variety of delicious desserts from Custard Flans to Banana Cream Pie and Mango Icebox Cake with the help of this easy-to-follow guide.

Basic Ingredients

Banana leaves are often used in Asian cuisine to wrap food or to line trays before cooking, much as waxed paper or aluminum foil are. This imparts a subtle fragrance to the food. Banana leaves should be passed over an open flame (be careful not to scorch them) for a few seconds before use to soften them, so that they do not crack when folded. Alternatively, dip the leaves in boiling water until they just start to soften. They are sold in rectangular sheets in provision shops and supermarkets and may be purchased frozen. If banana leaves are not available, substitute with waxed paper.

Coconut cream and **coconut milk** are used in many Asian desserts and curries. To obtain **fresh coconut cream** (which is normally used for desserts), grate the flesh of 1 coconut into a bowl (this yields about 3 cups of grated coconut flesh), add $^1/_2$ cup water and knead thoroughly a few times, then squeeze the mixture firmly in your fist or strain with a muslin cloth or cheese cloth. **Thick coconut milk** is obtained by the same method but by adding double the water to the grated flesh (about 1 cup instead of $^1/_2$ cup). **Thin coconut milk** (which is used for curries rather than desserts) is obtained by pressing the coconut a second time—adding 1 cup of water to the same grated coconut flesh and squeezing it again. Although freshly pressed milk has more flavor, coconut cream and milk are now widely sold canned or in packets that are quick, convenient and quite tasty. Canned or packet coconut cream or milk comes in varying consistencies depending on the brand, and you will need to try them out and adjust the thickness by adding water as needed. In general, you should add 1 cup of water to 1 cup of canned or packet coconut cream to obtain thick coconut milk, or 2 cups of water to 1 cup of coconut cream to obtain thin coconut milk. These mixing ratios are only general guides however. For best results, follow the package instructions.

Pandan leaves are long thin leaves used to add delicate fragrance and a light green color to cakes and desserts. Bottled pandan essence or vanilla essence may be used as a substitute.

Shortening is a solid vegetable fat that is used to give a flaky, tender texture to baked items. It is sold in tins or packets in supermarkets and is sometimes used as a substitute for butter.

Vanilla essence, sometimes known as vanilla extract, is widely used in cakes and to flavor desserts such as custards, ice creams and beverages. It is sold in small bottles in the baking section of supermarkets.

Young toasted rice, known in the Philippines as *pinipig*, is toasted in a pan to make it crunchy before use in desserts or as a topping. It can also be used as a cereal or as an accompaniment to thick hot chocolate. If young toasted rice is not available, any crispy rice cereal such as Rice Krispies may be used as a substitute.

Sweet Egg and Milk Bonbons

8 egg yolks
300 ml (1 $^1/_4$ cups)
  sweetened condensed
  milk
1 teaspoon lemon zest
300 g (1 $^1/_4$ cups) sugar
$^1/_4$ teaspoon cream of
  tartar

Makes about 30 bonbons
Preparation time: **5 mins**
  + 1$^3/_4$ hours for chilling,
  shaping and wrapping
  bonbons
Cooking time: **35 mins**

1 Combine the egg yolks and condensed milk in a double boiler. Add lemon zest. Cook over medium heat, stirring constantly, until very thick and mixture coats the back of a spoon when lifted, about 20 minutes. Chill for 1 hour for easier handling.

2 Grease hands and shape egg mixture into small balls, placing each ball into a greased pan.

3 In a saucepan, melt sugar and cream of tartar over low heat. Do not stir, otherwise sugar will crystallize. When the sugar becomes a brown syrup, stir then dip each ball into the syrup with a pair of tongs, swirling to coat evenly. Keep the syrup over low heat so it does not harden. Alternatively, if you do not wish to coat the bonbons in syrup, dust them lightly with sugar.

4 Put each coated ball into a greased pan and set aside to cool. Wrap individually in cellophane, if desired, before serving.

Mango Jam

4 large ripe mangoes
  (about 2 kg/4 lbs)
250 g (1 cup) sugar

Makes 2 cups
Preparation time: **5 mins**
Cooking time: **30 mins**

1 Cut the mangoes lengthwise and scrape out the mango flesh with a spoon. Slice or mash the mango very finely then measure out 400 g (2 cups) of fruit. Reserve the mango juice.

2 Combine the mango flesh, sugar and reserved mango juice in a medium saucepan. Bring to the boil and simmer over medium heat, stirring constantly, until mixture thickens and has the consistency of spreadable jam.

3 Remove from heat. Set aside to cool, then transfer to a clean container with cover. Mango Jam may be stored in a refrigerator for up to 1 week.

4 Serve as a spread for bread or crackers.

Sweetened Coconut (Macapuno)

250 g (1 cup) sugar
500 ml (2 cups) water
500 g (4 cups) grated
  young coconut or sport
  coconut flesh (see note)
1 tablespoon butter
1 teaspoon vanilla
  essence

Serves 6
Preparation time: **10 mins**
Cooking time: **15 mins**

1 Combine the sugar and water in a saucepan and bring to the boil. Simmer and cook until the liquid clears. Add the coconut flesh and simmer until the mixture thickens, about 5 minutes.
2 Stir in butter and vanilla essence. Heat through until the butter dissolves completely. Remove from the heat and set aside to cool before serving.

Sport coconuts *or macapuno, are smaller and have thicker and stickier flesh and less juice than regular coconuts. Regular coconuts may be used as a substitute. They taste similar to sport coconuts but give a different texture to this dish.*

Mini Custard Flans
(Tocino del Cielo)

190 g ($^3/_4$ cup) sugar
$^1/_4$ teaspoon cream of tartar
1 teaspoon lemon zest to serve (optional)
Whipped cream to serve (optional)

Custard Mixture
250 g (1 cup) sugar
5 egg yolks
1 egg
1 teaspoon lemon zest
$^1/_2$ teaspoon vanilla essence

1 Combine $^3/_4$ cup of sugar and cream of tartar in a saucepan. Simmer over low heat, without stirring, until sugar melts completely and forms a thin brown syrup, 15–20 minutes. When sugar has completely melted, divide equally between small muffin cups or flan molds. Spoon just enough of the sugar mixture to cover the bottoms of each container. Let stand until sugar hardens, about 1 minute.
2 To make the Custard Mixture, whisk the sugar, egg yolks and egg. Strain into a bowl. Add the lemon zest and vanilla essence and blend well. Set aside.
3 Divide the Custard Mixture equally between the muffin cups or flan molds, pouring the Custard Mixture over the hardened sugar mixture.
4 Place the muffin cups or flan molds in a steamer above a pan of boiling water. Cover with a tight fitting lid and steam over low heat for 10 minutes, or until firm, making sure the water does not enter the molds.
5 Remove from the heat and set aside to cool slightly. Run a knife gently around the edges of the molds to loosen the flans. Invert onto a serving platter. Serve with lemon zest and whipped cream if desired.

Serves 4
Preparation time: **20 mins**
Cooking time: **20 mins**

Coconut and Pandan Jellies in Sweet Cream

Combining the popular dessert flavors of coconut and pandan, this dessert has a rich, creamy dressing that enfolds cubes of gelatin and strips of fresh coconut.

2 young coconuts
4–6 pandan leaves,
  washed thoroughly
625 ml (2$^1/_2$ cups) water
90 g (3 oz) unflavored
  gelatin powder

Cream Dressing
170 g (6 oz) whipping
  cream
60 ml ($^1/_4$ cup) sweetened
  condensed milk

Serves 4–5
Preparation time: **10 mins**
  + 30 mins setting gelatin
  and 3 hours chilling salad
Cooking time: **20 mins**

1 Chop the tops off the coconuts, drain and reserve the juice. Scrape out the white part of the coconut flesh with a spoon and shred. Bring the reserved coconut juice to the boil, add the shredded coconut flesh and simmer for about 5 minutes. Drain and reserve the shredded coconut flesh and discard coconut juice.

2 In a separate saucepan, boil pandan leaves in 375 ml (1$^1/_2$ cups) of the water until water is infused with flavor and aroma of pandan leaves, about 10 minutes.

3 Discard pandan leaves, strain the pandan water then add enough fresh water to make 450 ml (1$^3/_4$ cups) of pandan liquid. Add gelatin powder to the liquid and stir to dissolve. Simmer over medium heat, stirring constantly, until liquid becomes clear, about 5 minutes. Pour into a 20-cm (8-in) dish and allow to set, about 15 minutes in refrigerator or 30 minutes at room temperature. Cut into small cubes.

4 To make the Cream Dressing, mix the cream and condensed milk in a bowl until smooth.

5 Toss pandan jelly cubes and young coconut strips in a separate bowl. Fold in Cream Dressing and chill for about 3 hours before serving.

Gelatin is sold in powdered form in small bottles and packets in supermarkets. As gelatin is obtained from animal tissue, it cannot be used in vegetarian dishes and should be substituted with agar-agar or gulaman. Pandan leaves are long thin leaves used to add delicate fragrance and a light green color to cakes and desserts. Bottled pandan essence or vanilla essence may be used as a substitute.

Sweet Stewed Bananas

1 kg (2 lbs) ripe cooking bananas
300 g (2 cups) dark brown sugar or palm sugar
1 liter (4 cups) water
1 teaspoon vanilla essence
500 ml (2 cups) fresh cream, evaporated milk or
  coconut cream
Crushed ice

1 Slice each banana diagonally into bite-sized pieces.
2 Combine sugar or palm sugar and water in a casserole dish or pot and bring to the boil, stirring occasionally until sugar dissolves.
3 Add the bananas and return to the boil. Lower heat and simmer until bananas are tender and the liquid becomes thick and syrupy, about 40 minutes. Skim off any impurities that rise to the top and discard.
4 Stir in vanilla essence and set aside to cool.
5 Spoon bananas and syrup into serving bowls. Add $^1/_4$ cup (60 ml) fresh cream or evaporated milk or coconut cream to each serving. Top with crushed ice.

Fresh coconut cream may be obtained by grating the flesh of 1 coconut into a bowl (this yields about 3 cups of grated coconut flesh). Add $^1/_2$ cup water and knead thoroughly a few times, then squeeze the mixture firmly in your fist or strain with a muslin cloth or cheese cloth.
Palm sugar ranges in color from golden brown to dark brown. It has a distinctive, maple-syrup flavor.

Serves 8–10
Preparation time: **5 mins**
Cooking time: **50 mins**

Rice Porridge with Corn
(Guinataang Mais)

200 g (1 cup) uncooked glutinous rice
1$^1/_4$ liters (5 cups) thin coconut milk
190 g ($^3/_4$ cup) sugar
1 teaspoon salt
1 x 425-g (15-oz) can whole kernel corn, drained or
  kernels from 2 fresh cobs of corn, steamed or boiled
  for 7 minutes
2 cups (500 ml) coconut cream, to serve

1 Combine the glutinous rice and coconut milk in a saucepan. Bring to the boil, then add sugar, salt and corn.
2 Simmer over very low heat until rice is tender and mixture has a porridge-like texture, about 15 minutes.
3 Pour into individual bowls and serve each bowl with 60 ml ($^1/_4$ cup) coconut cream.

Fresh coconut cream may be obtained by grating the flesh of 1 coconut into a bowl (this yields about 3 cups of grated coconut flesh). Add $^1/_2$ cup water and knead thoroughly a few times, then squeeze the mixture firmly in your fist or strain in a muslin cloth or cheese cloth.
Thin coconut milk is obtained by adding 2 cups of water to the same grated coconut flesh. Knead thoroughly a few times, then squeeze the mixture firmly in your fist or strain in a muslin cloth or cheesecloth. If you are using canned or packet coconut cream, add 2 cups of water to 1 cup of coconut cream to obtain thin coconut milk. This mixing ratio is only a general guide however. Different brands of packaged coconut cream vary in thickness, so follow the package instructions.

Serves 6–8
Preparation time: **5 mins**
Cooking time: **20 mins**

Fresh Jackfruit in Syrup

When a jackfruit tree is in full bloom, the huge oval-shaped fruits with their spiky covering hang heavily from the branches. The flesh inside the covering is a golden-yellow color. Jackfruits can be bought by the kilo, already peeled and sliced, from wet markets in many areas of Southeast Asia. They are also available canned.

1 kg (2 lbs) fresh or canned jackfruit flesh, sliced into short strips
500 ml (2 cups) water
500 g (2 cups) sugar

Serves 8
Preparation time: **10 mins**
Cooking time: **20 mins** +
  1 hour to cool jackfruit

1 Wash the jackfruit strips well. Bring 250 ml (1 cup) of the water to the boil in a saucepan. Drop the jackfruit strips into boiling water and cook over medium heat for 1 minute or until soft. With a slotted spoon, remove jackfruits from liquid and place in a heatproof bowl. Reserve liquid.

2 Add remaining 250 ml (1 cup) of water to the reserved liquid. Stir in sugar and simmer over medium heat for about 15 minutes or until sugar has completely dissolved and a slightly thick syrup has formed. Remove from the heat.

3 Pour syrup over jackfruit strips. Set aside for 1 hour to cool before serving. Serve at room temperature. Alternatively, chill in a refrigerator for a few hours before serving.

Sweet Banana and Jackfruit Spring Rolls

6 ripe cooking bananas
1 jackfruit (about 750 g/1$^1/_2$ lbs)
12 spring roll wrappers
75 g ($^1/_2$ cup) dark brown sugar or palm sugar (page 11)
60 ml ($^1/_4$ cup) water
250 ml (1 cup) cooking oil
1 cup toasted sesame seeds

1 Slice each banana in half lengthwise.
2 Skin and cut the jackfruit into 12 strips, equal in length to the sliced bananas.
3 Steam the spring roll wrappers for about 1 minute or until soft.
4 In a bowl, mix 1 tablespoon of the brown sugar with the water. To prepare the rolls, brush the edges of each wrapper with the sugar mixture. Place one banana and one jackfruit strip on each wrapper. Sprinkle with brown sugar, then roll each wrapper and press the edges together to seal.
5 Heat the oil in a wok or frying pan. Fry each roll over low heat until golden brown. Remove from pan and roll in toasted sesame seeds. Place on a paper towel to drain and serve warm.

Serves 6
Preparation time: **20 mins**
Cooking time: **10–15 mins**

Cassava Patties (Pichi Pichi)

450 g (2 cups) grated fresh cassava
250 ml (1 cup) water
125 g ($^1/_2$ cup) sugar
2–3 drops green food coloring (optional)
Grated coconut

1 Mix the cassava, water and sugar in a bowl. Pour into a blender and blend until mixture is smooth. Stir in food coloring if desired.
2 Pour the mixture into small molds or muffin pans and place in a steamer above a saucepan of boiling water. Cover with a tight-fitting lid and steam over medium heat for about 45 minutes, or until firm, making sure water does not touch the patties.
3 Set aside to cool, then remove from molds. Roll in grated coconut before serving.

Cassava is a long brown tuber that has a starchy white flesh. It is often grated and used to prepare cakes and snacks. It is available fresh in wet markets and supermarkets.

Makes 12 pieces
Preparation time: **20 mins**
Cooking time: **45 mins**

Glutinous Rice with Mango

600 g (3 cups) uncooked glutinous rice
750 ml (3 cups) thin coconut milk
500 ml (2 cups) coconut cream
190 g ($^3/_4$ cup) sugar
125 g (1 cup) grated mature coconut flesh
6–8 mangoes (3–4 kg/1$^1/_2$–2 lbs), sliced into wedges

1 In a large saucepan, combine the glutinous rice with the thin coconut milk and coconut cream. Bring to the boil, then simmer over medium heat, stirring occasionally, until the coconut mixture is absorbed and the rice is dry but sticky.
2 Spoon the rice onto a platter. Sprinkle sugar and grated coconut on top and serve with mango wedges.

Fresh coconut cream may be obtained by grating the flesh of 1 coconut into a bowl (this yields about 3 cups of grated coconut flesh). Add $^1/_2$ cup water and knead thoroughly a few times, then squeeze the mixture firmly in your fist or strain in a muslin cloth or cheese cloth.
Thin coconut milk is obtained by adding 2 cups of water to the same grated coconut flesh. Knead thoroughly a few times, then squeeze the mixture firmly in your fist or strain in a muslin cloth or cheesecloth. If you are using canned or packet coconut cream, add 2 cups of water to 1 cup of coconut cream to obtain thin coconut milk. This mixing ratio is only a general guide however. Different brands of packaged coconut cream vary in thickness, so follow the package instructions.

Serves 8–10
Preparation time: **5 mins**
Cooking time: **35–40 mins**

Glazed Bananas

Banana "cues" are often sold by street vendors in the streets of Manila. Perhaps their name derives from "barbecue", since the bananas are threaded on skewers, as are other fruits, vegetables and meats cooked on the barbecue. The brown sugar glaze adds sweetness, as well as a nice sheen, to the cooked bananas.

125 ml ($^1/_2$ cup) oil
4 ripe cooking bananas, peeled
75 g ($^1/_2$ cup) dark brown sugar or palm sugar
4 bamboo skewers

Serves 4
Preparation time: **5 mins**
Cooking time: **10 mins**

1 Heat the oil in a wok or large frying pan. Add the bananas to the wok, one or two at a time. Immediately sprinkle 1 tablespoon brown sugar or palm sugar evenly onto each banana.
2 Cook over low–medium heat until bananas are tender, about 10 minutes, stirring constantly. The sugar will melt and form a glaze on the bananas as they cook.
3 Thread bananas onto skewers and transfer to a greased tray. Set aside to cool before serving.

Palm sugar *ranges in color from golden brown to dark brown. It has a distinctive, maple-syrup flavor.*

Banana Cream Pie

2 ripe bananas
2 tablespoons lemon
 juice

Pie Crust
160 g (1$^{1}/_{4}$ cups) flour,
 plus extra for dusting
$^{1}/_{4}$ teaspoon salt
60 g ($^{1}/_{4}$ cup) chilled
 butter
50 g (2 tablespoons)
 chilled solid vegetable
 shortening
3–4 tablespoons iced
 water

Filling
500 ml (2 cups) cream
 or evaporated milk
6 tablespoons flour
60 g ($^{1}/_{4}$ cup) sugar
4 eggs
1 tablespoon butter
1 teaspoon vanilla
 essence
Whipped cream, to
 garnish (optional)

Serves 6–8
Preparation time: **20 mins**
 + 45 mins for freezing
 Pie Crust
Cooking time: **35–45 mins**

1 To make the Pie Crust, sift together flour and salt in a large bowl. Using a pastry blender or two knives, cut the butter and shortening into the flour until mixture resembles coarse breadcrumbs.

2 Sprinkle water gradually over the mixture, gathering the crumbs together until they form a ball. Sprinkle flour on waxed paper and wrap the gathered crumbs in the paper. Chill in a refrigerator for 30 minutes.

3 Sprinkle flour onto a smooth work surface. Roll out the chilled dough, starting from the center and lifting the rolling pin just before it reaches the edge. Roll the dough until it is 3 mm ($^{1}/_{8}$ in) thick and forms a circle, 5–8 cm (2–3 in) larger than a 23-cm (9-in) pie plate.

4 Lift the dough and ease it onto the plate. Press the dough firmly onto the bottom and sides of the plate. Make sure no air is trapped between the dough and the plate. Do not stretch the dough, or it will shrink.

5 Using kitchen scissors, trim excess dough from the edge of the pie plate, leaving a 4-cm (1$^{1}/_{2}$-in) over-hang. Fold the dough under its edges and flute or decorate edges as desired. Chill the dough in the freezer for 15 minutes.

6 Preheat an oven to 200°C (390°F).

7 Use a fork to pierce small holes in the surface and sides of the Pie Crust to allow steam to escape during baking. Line the crust with baking paper and fill with pie weights or dry beans.

8 Bake the Pie Crust in the preheated oven for 10–12 minutes. Transfer to a rack and remove baking paper and pie weights or dry beans. Bake for 5 more minutes, or until golden brown.

9 Slice the bananas into 1-cm ($^{1}/_{2}$-in) rounds. Sprinkle with lemon juice to prevent discoloration. Set aside.

10 To make the Filling, scald the cream or evaporated milk in a saucepan. Mix the flour, sugar and eggs in a bowl until smooth. Whisk in the cream or evaporated milk. Return to the saucepan and simmer, stirring to form a smooth mixture, about 20 minutes.

11 Blend in butter and vanilla essence. Spoon half of the Filling into the baked pie crust. Add bananas. Top with remaining Filling and whipped cream, if desired.

Egg Tarts

1 portion Pie Crust (see page 25)
4 large eggs
250 g (1 cup) sugar
$^1/_2$ teaspoon salt
625 ml (2$^1/_2$ cups) milk
1 teaspoon vanilla essence

1 Make the Pie Crust according to steps 1–2 on page 25. Divide the pie dough into 8 equal portions. Sprinkle flour onto a smooth work surface. Roll out each portion of dough until it is 3 mm ($^1/_8$ in) thick and forms a circle.
2 Press each portion of the dough onto the sides and bottoms of the custard cups. Make sure no air is trapped between the dough and each cup.
3 Preheat oven to 220°C (425°F).
4 In a large mixing bowl, beat together the eggs, sugar, salt, milk and vanilla essence. Strain and pour into each Pie Crust.
5 Bake in the preheated oven for 30 minutes, or until a knife inserted into the center of each tart comes out clean.

Serves 8
Preparation time: 15 mins + 45 mins for chilling and
    freezing pie crust
Cooking time: 30 mins

Quick Jelly Rolls (Pionono)

4 eggs
250 g (1 cup) sugar
125 g (1 cup) flour
1 teaspoon baking powder
$^1/_2$ teaspoon salt
3 tablespoons melted
  butter
Icing sugar for dusting
125 ml ($^1/_2$ cup) straw-
  berry or raspberry jam

Serves 8–10
Preparation time: **20 mins**
Cooking time: **20 mins**

1 Preheat an oven to 180°C (350°F).
2 Beat eggs until bright yellow and thick. Gradually stir in the sugar. Sift flour, baking powder and salt then fold into the egg mixture.
3 Scoop out one cup of the egg-flour mixture and fold into the butter. Fold back into the egg-flour mixture.
4 Pour into a baking tray lined with waxed paper. Bake in preheated oven for 20 minutes.
5 Sprinkle the icing sugar onto a piece of waxed paper. Invert the sponge cake onto the paper, then peel off the top sheet of waxed paper. Invert again into the waxed paper. Set aside to cool.
6 When cooled, spread jam on the top of the sponge cake then roll tightly. Dust the roll with powdered sugar. Cut into thin slices to serve.

Sift the flour, baking powder and salt into the egg mixture.

Invert sponge cake onto a piece of waxed paper sprinkled with icing sugar.

Peel off the top layer of waxed paper.

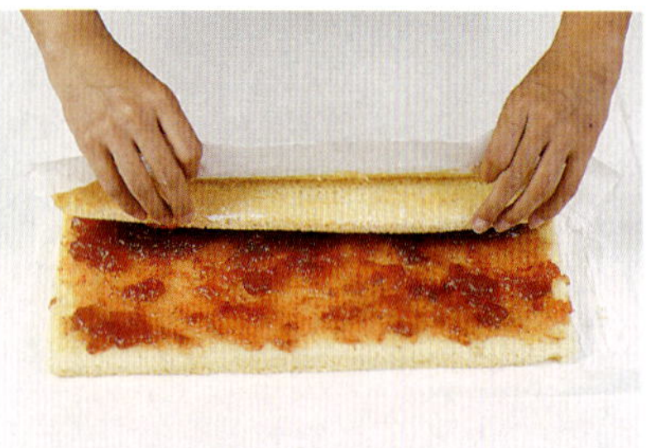

When cooled, spread jam on the top of the sponge cake then roll.

Calamansi Lime Pie

The humble calamansi lime adds a tang to this rich, creamy pie, while the crust made from finger biscuits is wonderfully innovative.

Pie Crust

75 g (³/₄ cup) finger biscuit crumbs

3 tablespoons sugar

60 ml (¹/₄ cup) melted butter

Filling

60 ml (¹/₄ cup) water

1 tablespoon unflavored gelatin powder

500 ml (2 cups) whipping cream, well chilled

300 ml (1¹/₄ cups) condensed milk

60 ml (¹/₄ cup) freshly squeezed calamansi lime juice

2–3 drops green food coloring

Whipped cream for topping (optional)

Serves 8

Preparation time: **40 mins + 6 hours for chilling**

Cooking time: **10 mins**

1 Preheat an oven to 180°C (350°F).

2 To make the Pie Crust, mix the biscuit crumbs, sugar and melted butter. Press mixture into a 23-cm (9-in) pie plate and chill for about 15 minutes. Bake crust for about 5 minutes in the preheated oven. Set aside to cool.

3 To make the Filling, pour water into a small saucepan and sprinkle unflavored gelatin powder on top. Set aside for 5 minutes to allow gelatin granules to swell. Heat over low heat, stirring until liquid clears and gelatin is completely dissolved, about 3 minutes. Set aside.

4 Beat the whipping cream with a mixer at medium speed for 5 minutes. Slowly add condensed milk and lime juice and beat to blend, about 2 minutes. Add the food coloring and the gelatin mixture and beat until mixture is smooth and an even light green color. Chill for 5–10 minutes, or until partially set.

5 Spoon Filling into the cooled Pie Crust. Chill for 6 hours before serving, topped with whipped cream, if desired.

__Calamansi limes__ are small and yellow-green in color. They are often used in marinades and dips and also add an aromatic citrus flavor to desserts.
__Finger biscuits__ are often used to add a crunchy texture to desserts. They are sold in packets in supermarkets. If finger biscuits are not available, substitute with pound cake or savioardi biscuits.

Delicious Young Coconut Pie

Pie Crust

300 g (2$^1/_2$ cups) flour, plus extra for dusting

$^1/_2$ teaspoon salt

125 g ($^1/_2$ cup) chilled butter

75 g ($^1/_3$ cup) chilled solid vegetable shortening

6 tablespoons iced water

2 tablespoons milk or cream

1 tablespoon sugar

Filling

300 g (2$^1/_2$ cups) sliced young coconut meat

250 g (1 cup) sugar

30 g ($^1/_3$ cup) cornstarch

125 ml ($^1/_2$ cup) young coconut juice

125 ml ($^1/_2$ cup) milk

1 tablespoon butter

1 teaspoon vanilla essence

Serves 6–8

Preparation time: **10 mins** + **40 mins for pie crusts**

Cooking time: **40 mins**

1 To make the Pie Crust, sift together flour and salt in a large bowl. With a pastry blender or knife, cut butter and shortening into the flour until mixture resembles coarse breadcrumbs. Sprinkle water over the mixture, gathering the crumbs together until they form a ball. Wrap in waxed paper sprinkled with flour and chill in a refrigerator for about 30 minutes.

2 Remove half of the chilled dough from the refrigerator. Sprinkle flour onto a smooth work surface. Roll out the chilled dough, starting from the center and ending just before the edge (lift the rolling pin before reaching the edge). Rotate dough at regular intervals to form a circle. Continue rolling the dough until it is 3 mm ($^1/_8$ in) thick and forms a circle, 5–8 cm (2–3 in) larger than a 23-cm (9-in) pie plate.

3 Lift the dough and ease it gently onto a pie plate. Press firmly on bottom and sides of the plate. Make sure there is no air trapped between the dough and the plate. Do not stretch the dough or it will shrink.

4 Trim the dough with kitchen scissors, leaving 4 cm (1$^1/_2$ in) hanging over the rim of the pie plate. Fold the excess dough under its edges. Freeze for 15 minutes and preheat an oven to 200°C (400°F).

5 To prepare the Filling, combine the sliced coconut meat, sugar, cornstarch, coconut juice and milk in a saucepan. Heat, stirring constantly until slightly thickened. Stir in butter and vanilla essence. Cook over very low heat for 5 more minutes, stirring until the mixture is smooth.

6 Spoon the Filling onto the Pie Crust. Take out the remaining chilled dough from the refrigerator and roll out as in step 2. Place on top of the Filling and press the edges of the top crust and lower crust together to seal. Alternatively, cut the chilled dough into long strips and arranged to form a lattice pattern on top of the Filling, as shown in the photograph.

7 Flute or decorate edge as desired. Cut slits at center of top crust to allow steam to escape during baking. Brush the top of the pie with milk or cream and sprinkle lightly with sugar. Bake in preheated oven for 20 minutes or until crust is golden.

Cashew Tarts

Crust

- 250 g (2 cups) flour
- 2$\frac{1}{2}$ tablespoons sugar
- $\frac{1}{4}$ teaspoon baking powder
- $\frac{1}{4}$ teaspoon salt
- 125 g ($\frac{1}{2}$ cup) butter
- 1 egg yolk, slightly beaten
- 1 tablespoon lemon juice
- 6 tablespoons iced water

Cashew Filling

- 3 eggs
- 250 g (1 cup) sugar
- 250 ml (1 cup) maple syrup, corn syrup or pancake syrup
- 2 tablespoons melted butter, plus extra for greasing molds
- 1 teaspoon vanilla essence
- 150 g (1 cup) finely chopped cashew nuts

1 To make the Crust, sift together flour, sugar, baking powder and salt in a bowl. Cut in butter with a pastry blender or knife until the mixture resembles coarse breadcrumbs. Add egg yolk and lemon juice. Blend in water, 1 tablespoon at a time, until the dough can be formed into a ball. Wrap in waxed paper sprinkled with flour and chill for 30 minutes.

2 To make the Cashew Filling, combine all the filling ingredients and set aside.

3 Preheat oven to 180°C (350°F). Sprinkle flour onto a smooth work surface. When Crust has been chilled for 30 minutes, roll it out onto floured work surface using a rolling pin, until it is 3 mm ($\frac{1}{8}$ in) thick. Use an inverted tart mold or knife to cut out the dough. Combine and roll any remaining dough and cut out. Brush tart molds with melted butter and place the cut out pieces of dough into each mold.

4 Pour about 1 tablespoon of the Filling into each mold. Arrange tarts on a baking sheet and bake in preheated oven for 20–25 minutes or until pastry is light brown and filling is just firm (it will continue to firm up for a few minutes after it has been removed from oven). Remove from molds and wrap in cellophane if desired, or store in an airtight container if not eating immediately.

Makes about 20 tarts
Preparation time: **30 mins + 30 mins chilling**
Baking time: **20–25 mins**

Butter Cream Silvanas

Icing
250 g (1 cup) butter
190 g (³/₄ cup) sugar
185 ml (³/₄ cup) milk

Biscuits
5 egg whites
¹/₄ teaspoon cream of
  tartar
250 g (1 cup) sugar
60 g (¹/₂ cup) flour
75 g (³/₄ cup) ground
  toasted cashew nuts
¹/₄ cup pounded finger
  biscuits

Makes about 12 silvanas
Preparation time:
  Silvanas 20 mins +
  5 hours chilling
Baking time: **10 mins**

1 To make the Icing, beat the butter in an electric mixer until light and fluffy. Mix the sugar and milk in a separate bowl. Gradually beat the milk mixture into the butter, beating until mixture is of a spreadable consistency. Chill for 1 hour in the refrigerator.
2 Preheat an oven to 180°C (350°F).
3 To make the Biscuits, beat the egg whites and cream of tartar until soft peaks form. Add sugar gradually and continue beating until slightly stiff.
4 Fold in flour and nuts. Scoop out mixture with an ice-cream scoop and place on a greased and floured biscuit tray. Flatten mounds and smoothen tops with a spatula. Bake in preheated oven for 10 minutes.
5 Cool on a biscuit tray for 1 minute, then transfer to a dry plate. Set aside to cool.
6 Spread the Icing on one side of half the biscuits. Top with remaining biscuits. Spread icing on surface of the biscuits and sprinkle with pounded finger biscuits. Chill for 4 hours before serving.

***Finger biscuits** are often used to add a crunchy texture to desserts. They are sold in packets in supermarkets. If finger biscuits are not available, substitute with pound cake or savioardi biscuits.*

Toasted Rice Ice Cream
(Pinipig Ice Cream)

75 g (³/₄ cup) toasted young rice (*pinipig*) or 25 g
   (³/₄ cup) crispy rice cereal (see note)
500 ml (2 cups) chilled whipping cream
500 ml (2 cups) sweetened condensed milk
1 teaspoon vanilla essence
Chocolate fudge topping

1 Lightly pound the rice cereal or toasted young rice to break it into smaller pieces.

2 Beat the chilled cream in a chilled mixing bowl until fluffy. Add condensed milk and continue beating until well blended. Reserve 2 tablespoons of the pounded rice cereal or toasted young rice. Add remaining rice cereal or toasted young rice to the cream mixture and stir in vanilla essence.

3 Pour the cereal-cream mixture into a 2 liter bowl or a loaf pan and freeze for 6–8 hours or until slightly firm. Pour chocolate fudge topping on top and sprinkle with the reserved rice cereal or toasted young rice. Return to freezer and let set for about 12 hours.

***Toasted young rice** or pinipig is toasted for five minutes until it is light brown before being served or used in desserts. In the Philippines, it is available from wet markets and supermarkets; substitute with a crispy rice cereal, such as Rice Krispies, if unavailable.*

Serves 10–12
Preparation time: **20 mins**
Freezing time: **18–20 hours**

Purple Yam Ice Cream

3 purple yams (*ube*), (about 450 g/1 lb)
250 ml (1 cup) milk
500 ml (2 cups) chilled whipped cream
250 ml (1 cup) sweetened condensed milk
2 tablespoons sugar

1 Peel the yams and boil in water until softened.
Drain, set aside to cool, then grate yams to make 225 g
($1^1/_2$ cups).
2 Combine grated yam and milk and pour into an
electric blender. Blend until smooth and set aside.
3 Beat the whipped cream in a chilled mixing bowl
until fluffy. Add condensed milk and sugar and mix
well. Beat in the yam mixture and continue beating
until mixture is smooth.
4 Pour into a 2-liter glass mold or a loaf pan. Freeze
for about 12 hours or until firm. If desired, top with
Macapuno (see page 5) before serving.

***Purple yams** are tubers with grayish brown skins and
purple flesh. They taste sweet and are sold fresh in
supermarkets or wet markets.*

Serves 8–10
Preparation time: **35 mins**
Freezing time: **12 hours**

Homemade Avocado Ice Cream

While others use avocado in their salads and sandwiches, it is made into a delicious sweet ice cream in the Philippines. Mixed with sugar and milk, it makes for a rich creamy dessert.

3–4 ripe avocadoes
  (about 1 kg/2 lbs)
190 g ($^3/_4$ cup) sugar
250 ml (1 cup) milk
Whipped cream for
  topping (optional)

Serves 6
Preparation time: **15 mins**
Freezing time: **24 hours**

1 Scoop out avocado flesh and mash coarsely. Purée avocado flesh in a blender, add sugar and milk and blend mixture until smooth.
2 Pour the mixture into a 2 liter container and freeze for 24 hours.
3 Scoop into glass dessert bowls and top with whipped cream if desired.

Frozen Young Coconut

As some coconuts yield more juice than others, between two and four young coconuts will be required for this recipe. You can always freeze the excess juice and add more coconut to the frozen juice. Serve for dessert or as an afternoon snack.

2–4 young coconuts
125 g ($^1/_2$ cup) sugar

1 Remove the tops of the young coconuts with a chopper and pour the coconut juice into a pitcher. You should have about 1 liter (4 cups) of juice. Scrape out the white coconut flesh. Put the coconut flesh into a covered container and refrigerate until ready to use.
2 Stir sugar into the coconut juice. Pour into desired mold or container. Put in the freezer for 1–2 hours until slightly set, then stir in the coconut meat. Return to freezer and freeze for 24 hours, or until firm.
3 Crush the frozen dessert with an ice pick, scoop out, then serve in dessert bowls.

Serves 8
Preparation time: **20 mins**
Freezing time: **24 hours**

Frozen Fruit Salad

A favorite at parties and during the holiday season, this frozen treat combines canned and fresh fruits with a sweet, creamy sauce. Make sure you thaw it in the refrigerator for about 1–2 hours before serving.

4 x 450 g (16 oz) cans fruit cocktail

2 x 450 g cans (16 oz) sliced peaches

1 red apple

1 tablespoon fresh lemon juice

1 tablespoon lemon zest (optional)

8 whole maraschino cherries to garnish (optional)

Cream Sauce

1 220-g (8-oz) pack cream cheese, softened

500 ml (2 cups) double cream

300 ml (1^1/$_4$ cups) sweetened condensed milk

1 Drain fruit cocktail and peaches overnight to make sure fruits are dry. If desired, reserve about 8 peach slices for garnish and store in a refrigerator. Cut the remaining peaches into bite-sized pieces, equal in size to the fruit cocktail. Peel the apple and cut into cubes of similar size. Toss apple cubes in lemon juice to prevent discoloration.

2 To prepare the Cream Sauce, whisk the cream cheese until smooth. Stir in the double cream and condensed milk until smooth.

3 Combine drained fruit cocktail, peaches and apples in a large bowl. Fold in the Cream Sauce and lemon zest, if desired, mixing thoroughly so that the fruits are evenly coated. Pour into a large bowl. Garnish with reserved peach slices and maraschino cherries, if desired. Cover and freeze for 12 hours.

4 Thaw in the refrigerator 1–2 hours before serving.

Serves 12–15
Preparation time: **15 mins + 12 hours for draining**
Freezing time: **12 hours**

Almond Jelly with Lychees

This dessert is served in many Chinese restaurants in Asia. It combines gelatin cubes flavored with milk and almond extract with lychees. Make sure this dessert is well chilled before serving.

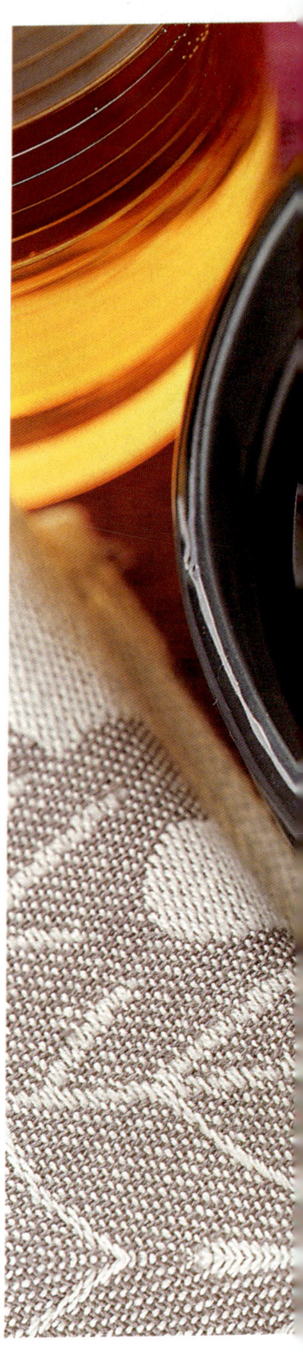

500 ml (2 cups) fresh milk
60 g ($^1/_4$ cup) sugar
1 x 500 g (18 oz) can lychees in heavy syrup
2 tablespoons unflavored gelatin powder
1 teaspoon almond extract

1 Combine the milk and sugar in a saucepan. Bring to the boil then lower heat and simmer for 2 minutes or until sugar dissolves. Set aside to cool.
2 Drain the canned lychees into a bowl and reserve the syrup. Measure out 2 tablespoons of the reserved syrup and sprinkle the gelatin on top of it. Bring 2 more tablespoons of the reserved syrup to the boil, then pour over gelatin mixture. Stir until gelatin is completely dissolved then pour into the milk mixture. Stir in almond extract.
3 Pour milk mixture into a 20-cm (8-in) square cake tin and chill in a refrigerator for 2 hours, or until set. When the milk mixture is set, cut into cubes and add lychees. Pour in remaining syrup and chill before serving.

__Almond extract__ or almond essence, is often used in cookies and cakes. If almond extract is not available, substitute with vanilla essence.

Serves 4–6
Preparation time: **15 mins + 1–2 hours for setting**

Mango Icebox Cake

6 large ripe mangoes
  (about 3 kg/6 lbs)
75 finger biscuits
500 ml (2 cups) canned
  mango juice
3 225-g (8-oz) packs
  cream cheese
500 ml (2 cups) double
  cream
375 g (3 cups) powdered
  sugar

Serves 8–10
Preparation time: **40 mins**
Chilling time: **4–5 hours**

1 Peel mangoes and slice into wedges then set aside. Dip 25 of the finger biscuits one at a time, into the mango juice. Arrange in a 30 x 20 x 5 cm (12 x 8 x 2 in) cake tin, with the tops of the biscuits facing down.
2 In an electric mixer, beat together cream cheese and double cream. Gradually add sugar and beat until mixture is smooth. Divide the cream cheese mixture into three equal portions.
3 Spread a layer of the cream cheese mixture over the finger biscuits. Arrange one-third of the mango wedges over the cream cheese mixture. Dip 25 more finger biscuits, one at a time, in mango juice and layer over the mangoes. Spread another layer of the cream cheese mixture on the finger biscuits and arrange another layer of mangoes on top.
4 Dip remaining finger biscuits in mango juice and arrange on top of mangoes. Spread remaining cream cheese mixture on the finger biscuits. Arrange remaining mango wedges on top. Chill for 4–5 hours, or until firm, before serving.

***Finger biscuits** are often used to add a crunchy texture to desserts. They are sold in packets in supermarkets. If finger biscuits are not available, substitute with pound cake or savioardi biscuits.*

Powdered Milk Cookies
(Polvoron)

Children love to eat these sweet, powdery cookies, but they're a great dessert for adults too. Chilling the mixture for about 30 minutes makes it easier to shape into molds.

125 g (1 cup) sifted flour
125 g (4 oz) butter, slightly softened
125 g ($^1/_2$ cup) sugar
60 g ($^3/_4$ cup) full-cream powdered milk
1 teaspoon vanilla essence

1 Dry roast the flour in a non-stick pan, stirring continuously for 5 minutes, or until flour turns light brown. Remove from heat and set aside to cool.
2 Mix the butter, sugar and powdered milk in a bowl. Add the flour and vanilla essence and mix until well combined. Chill the mixture for 30 minutes.
3 Use a muffin tin or polvoron molder (see picture), to mold the mixture. Wrap in decorative Japanese paper if desired, and chill for 2 hours, or until firm, before serving.

Serves 6–8
Preparation: **2–3 hours**

Iced Melon Ball Dessert

There's nothing more refreshing on a hot day than a glass of iced honeydew or rockmelon (cantaloupe) sweetened with sugar.

1 honeydew or rockmelon (cantaloupe) (about 1 kg/2 lbs)
300 g (1 ¹/₄ cups) sugar
1 liter (4 cups) cold water
Ice cubes

1 Scoop out the honeydew or rockmelon flesh with a melon baller, reserving any juice if desired, and set aside.
2 Combine the sugar and water in a pitcher. Stir until the sugar dissolves.
3 Spoon the honeydew or rockmelon flesh and reserved juice, if desired, into the pitcher. Stir in ice cubes.
4 Pour into glasses and serve.

Serves 4
Preparation time: **10 mins**

Sweet Sago Parfait

3¹/₂ liters (14 cups) water, plus additional for rinsing
100 g (¹/₂ cup) dried sago pearls (see page 59)
90-g (3-oz) gelatin or red unflavored *gulaman*
300 g (2 cups) dark brown sugar or palm sugar (page 11)
Crushed ice

1 Bring 1 liter (4 cups) of the water to the boil. Add sago pearls to the boiling water and simmer for 15 minutes, stirring constantly to keep the sago from sticking. Drain sago and rinse in tap water several times to cool. Transfer sago to a container and add enough water to soak the sago completely. Refrigerate for 12 hours or overnight.

2. The next day, boil sago in another 1 liter (4 cups) water for 10 minutes, stirring frequently. Drain sago and rinse again in tap water several times. Transfer sago to a container and add enough fresh water to soak the sago completely. Refrigerate for 3 hours or until white parts disappear. Rinse sago before serving.

3 Pour 500 ml (2 cups) water into a saucepan, sprinkle gelatin on top and stir until it is dissolved. Heat over low heat, stirring until liquid is clear. Pour into a 20-cm (8-in) cake tin and set for 30 minutes at room temperature or 15 minutes in the refrigerator.

4 In another saucepan, combine sugar and 1 liter (4 cups) of water. Simmer over medium heat, stirring until sugar dissolves and mixture becomes a light syrup. Cut the gelatin into small cubes and set aside.

5 For each serving, spoon ¹/₂ cup of the gelatin cubes into a glass and add ¹/₂ cup cooked sago. Pour in 1 cup of the syrup and top with crushed ice.

Gulaman is the Filipino term for agar-agar. It is available in powdered form or in strips and is sold in supermarkets and grocery stores.

Serves 4
Preparation time: **35 mins + 15 hours for soaking sago**
Cooking time: **10 mins**

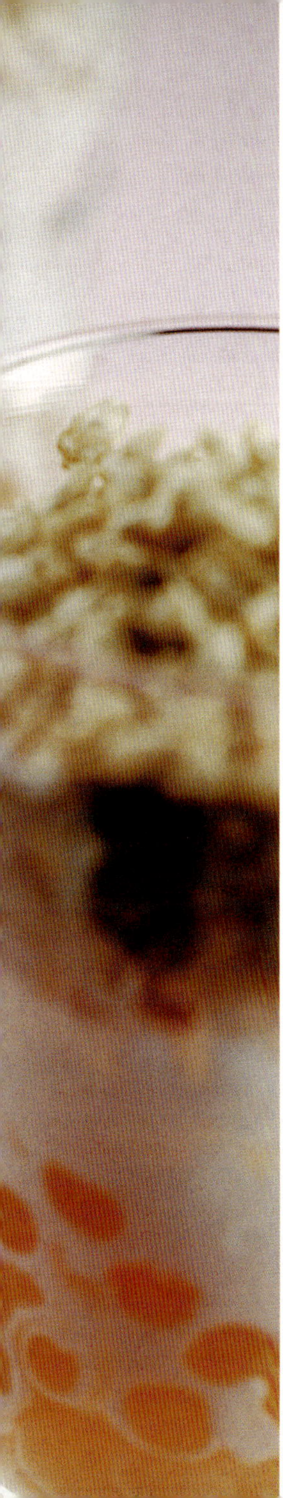

Sago in Coconut Syrup with Toasted Rice (Guinomis)

100 g (¹/₂ cup) dried sago pearls
3 liters (12 cups) water, plus additional for rinsing
300 g (2 cups) dark brown sugar or palm sugar (page 11)
250 ml (1 cup) coconut cream (page 11)
Crushed ice
100 g (1 cup) crispy rice cereal or 35 g (1 cup) toasted young rice (*pinipig*) (see page 40)

1 Bring 1 liter (4 cups) of water to the boil. Add sago pearls to the boiling water and simmer for 15 minutes, stirring constantly to keep the sago from sticking. Drain sago and rinse in water to cool, then add enough water to the container to soak the sago completely. Refrigerate for 12 hours or overnight.
2 The next day, boil sago in 1 liter (4 cups) water for 10 minutes, stirring frequently. Drain sago and rinse again in tap water several times. Transfer sago to a container and add enough fresh water to soak the sago completely. Refrigerate for about three hours or until white parts disappear. Rinse sago before serving.
3 In a saucepan combine brown sugar and 1 liter (4 cups) water. Heat over medium heat, stirring for 5–10 minutes, or until sugar dissolves and the mixture becomes syrupy. Remove from heat and cool.
4 For each serving, pour about 60 ml (¹/₄ cup) coconut cream into a glass. Add 100 g (¹/₂ cup) cooked sago. Add 1 cup of the sugar syrup and crushed ice and top with crispy rice cereal or toasted young rice.

Sago pearls are tiny dried balls of sago obtained by grinding the pith of the sago palm to a paste and pressing it through a sieve. It is glutinous, with little taste, and is often used in Asian desserts. Sago pearls should not be confused with fresh sago, which is starchy and sticky.

Serves 4
Preparation time: **10 mins**
Cooking time: **5–10 mins (for making the syrup)**

Mango Pudding

3 large ripe mangoes (about 1$^1/_2$ kg/3 lbs)
1$^1/_2$ tablespoons unflavored gelatin powder
125 ml ($^1/_2$ cup) cold water
125 ml ($^1/_2$ cup) boiling water
190 g ($^3/_4$ cup) sugar
180 ml ($^3/_4$ cup) cream or unsweetened evaporated milk
1 teaspoon vanilla essence
Whipped cream, for topping (optional)
1 small mango, sliced into wedges, for topping (optional)

1 Scoop out the mango flesh and purée in a blender. Soften gelatin powder in cold water, then stir in the boiling water and mix until gelatin is dissolved. Set aside to cool. Combine the gelatin and mango purée and mix thoroughly.

2 Stir sugar and cream or evaporated milk in a bowl until sugar is dissolved. Add to mango-gelatin mixture. Stir in the vanilla essence.

3 Pour into dessert bowls and chill for 6 hours, or until firm.

4 Top with whipped cream and mango wedges, if desired, before serving.

Serves 6
Preparation time: **15 mins**
Setting time: **6 hours**

Layered Fruit Cocktail Cake (Crema de Fruta)

50–60 finger biscuits or
   sliced pound cake
2 x 450 g (1 lb) cans fruit
   cocktail, well drained,
   syrup reserved

Filling
250 g (1 cup) sugar
40 g ($^1/_3$ cup) flour
560 ml ($2^1/_4$ cups) cream
   or unsweetened evapo-
   rated milk
180 ml ($^3/_4$ cup) water
3 egg yolks
2 tablespoons butter
1 teaspoon vanilla
   essence

Chocolate Sauce
375 ml ($1^1/_2$ cups)
   whipping cream
340 g (12 oz) semi-sweet
   chocolate chips

Glaze
2 tablespoons unflavored
   gelatin powder
125 ml ($^1/_2$ cup) cold
   water
125 ml ($^1/_2$ cup) boiling
   water

Serves 10–12
Preparation time: **25 mins**
Cooking time: **35–40 mins**
   + 6 hours for settting
Assembly time: **15 mins**

1 To prepare the Filling, combine the sugar and flour in a saucepan and mix well. Pour in cream or evaporated milk, and water and cook over medium heat, stirring until mixture thickens slightly, about 10 minutes.
2 Remove from heat and add yolks, one at a time, mixing well after each yolk is added. Return to heat and continue cooking until mixture becomes thick and of spreadable consistency, 10–15 minutes. Stir in butter and vanilla essence. Set aside to cool.
3 To make the Chocolate Sauce, heat whipping cream in a saucepan. Just before the cream mixture starts to boil, turn off heat and stir in the chocolate chips.
4 Continue stirring until all the chocolate has melted completely.
5 To assemble, dip 20–25 finger biscuits or pound cake slices, one at a time, in the reserved fruit cocktail syrup. Arrange the biscuits in a 30 x 20 x 5 cm (12 x 8 x 2 in) dish, with the top side face down.
6 Spread the cooled Filling onto the finger biscuits or sliced pound cake. Arrange half the drained fruit cocktail on top of the Filling. Dip remaining biscuits or cake slices, one at a time, in reserved syrup and layer on top of fruit, top sides facing up.
7 Spread chocolate sauce on the finger biscuits or cake slices. Arrange remaining fruit cocktail on top.
8 To make the Glaze, sprinkle gelatin powder onto the cold water and set aside. Let stand for 5 minutes. Pour in boiling water and stir until gelatin powder dissolves. Set aside to cool then pour on top of the assembled cake. Leave in a refrigerator for 6 hours or until set.

***Finger biscuits** are often used to add a crunchy texture to desserts. They are sold in packets in super-markets. If finger biscuits are not available, substitute with pound cake or savioardi biscuits.*

List of Recipes